NOW YOU CAN READ.
JONAH

STORY RETOLD BY LEONARD MATTHEWS

ILLUSTRATED BY HARRY BISHOP

Library of Congress Cataloging in Publication Data

Matthews, Leonard.
  Jonah.

  (Now you can read—Bible stories)
  Summary: Retells the Bible story of Jonah, the
prophet who was swallowed by a whale as punishment
for disobeying God.
  1. Jonah (Biblical prophet)—Juvenile literature.
2. Bible.   O.T.—Biography—Juvenile literature.
3. Bible stories, Juvenile—O.T.   Jonah.   [1. Jonah
(Biblical prophet)   2. Bible stories—O.T.]
I. Title.   II. Series.
BS580.J55M33   1984   224'.92'0924   [B]   84-15128
ISBN 0-86625-306-8

GROLIER ENTERPRISES CORP.

NOW YOU CAN READ. . . .
JONAH

A prophet is a person who can pass
on messages from God. Long ago
there lived a prophet named Jonah.
He lived in the land of Judah. In
those days southern Israel was
called Judah.
One day God spoke to Jonah.

"Go to the city of Nineveh," God said. "Tell the people there they are being very bad. I am very angry with them. They shall be punished."

Nineveh was the most important city in the country of Assyria. Assyria lay to the north of Judah. Some time before, Assyria had conquered Judah.

God was now asking Jonah to tell the people who had conquered Judah that his God was angry with them. Jonah was afraid. He boarded a ship.

The ship that Jonah boarded was not going to Assyria. It was going in the opposite direction. Jonah knew the ship was not going to Nineveh. He was disobeying God.

God knew that Jonah was disobeying Him. Soon after the ship had set sail, a great storm started.

The ship was carrying a heavy cargo. Because of this, the ship was in danger of being sunk by the huge waves. The sailors started to throw the cargo overboard. Then they prayed to their gods to save them.

The storm kept getting stronger.
The captain of the ship shouted to
Jonah: "Our gods are not helping us.
Try praying to your God. Perhaps
He can save us."
Jonah prayed to God.

The storm still raged. "One of us
has offended his God," shouted the
captain. "Let us throw dice to find
out who it is. The one who loses, is
the one who has made his God angry."

The sailors threw dice.
Jonah was the unlucky man. The
sailors seized him. "Who are you?
Where do you come from?" they cried.

"I am a Hebrew from Judah," replied Jonah. The sailors were even more afraid. They had heard of the great God of the Hebrews.

"Fear not," called out Jonah. "God has sent this storm to punish me – not you – for disobeying Him."

"You are the one who is to blame for all the danger we are in," the captain shouted. "What should we do with you so that your God will calm the sea?"

"You must throw me into the sea," Jonah told the captain. "Then the storm will stop."

At first, the sailors did not want to do this.

By now, the ship was close to sinking. The sailors did all they could to save it. They even promised that they would serve Jonah's God. The waves got even higher.

"There is nothing else we can do," cried the captain. "We must do as this man says." The sailors all agreed with the captain. They took hold of Jonah and threw him into the sea. Jonah sank from sight.

At once the great wind died down
and the rain stopped falling.
The sky cleared and the sea
became calm again. The grateful
sailors knelt down. Again, they
promised that they would pray to
the God of the Hebrews.

Meanwhile, what had happened to poor Jonah? By God's command a great fish had swallowed him. It has been thought that the fish must have been a whale.

Jonah did not die when the fish swallowed him. He lived inside the fish.

In the Bible we are told that
Jonah was inside the big fish
"for three days and nights."
In the Hebrew language, this
means any short space of time.

Jonah prayed to God. He asked for
forgiveness and he promised to obey.
God heard him. He ordered the fish
to throw Jonah out of its mouth
onto dry land. God spoke to Jonah
again.

"Do as I tell you," said God. "Go to the wicked city of Nineveh. Tell the people they have forty days to give up their evil ways. If they do not, I will destroy them and their city." So Jonah went to Nineveh. The people surprised him. They listened to him and said they believed in his God.

Even the King of Nineveh agreed to
worship God. Later, God spoke to
Jonah. "The people are like
children," He said. "They do not
know right from wrong. Now they
believe in me. I have saved them."
Jonah learned that the orders of God
must be obeyed. He also learned that
the Lord is merciful.

All these appear in the pages of the story. Can you find them?

King of Nineveh

Jonah

ship's captain

ship

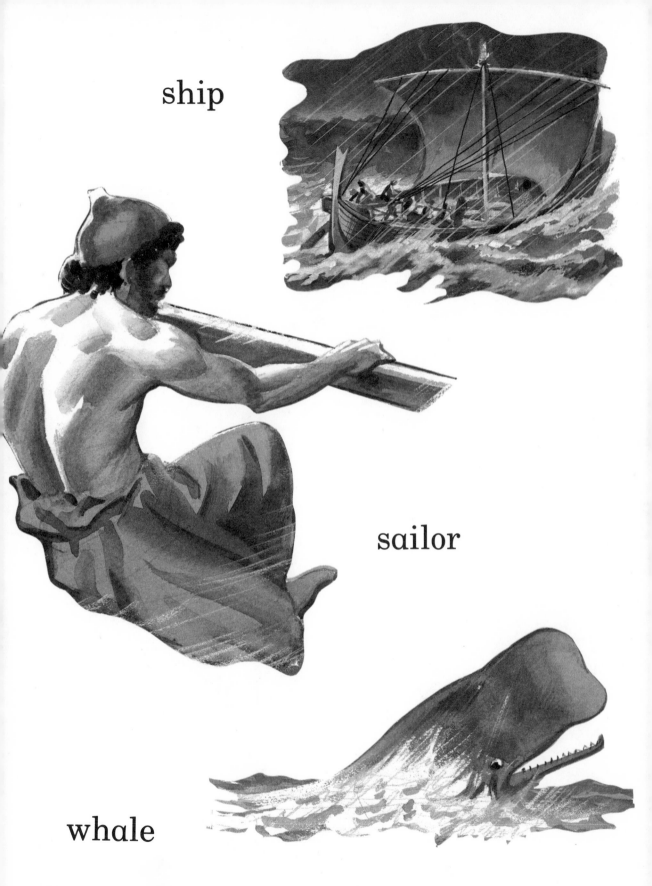

sailor

whale

Now tell the story in your own words.